Iguanas

and Other Lizards

Book Author: Karen Ingebretsen
For World Book:
Editorial: Paul A. Kobasa, Scott Thomas, Christine Sullivan
Research: Cheryl Graham
Graphics and Design: Sandra Dyrlund, Brenda Tropinski
Photos: Tom Evans
Permissions: Janet Peterson
Indexing: David Pofelski
Proofreading: Tina Ramirez
Pre-press and Manufacturing: Carma Fazio, Anne Fritzinger, Steve Hueppchen

For information about other World Book publications, visit our Web site at http://www.worldbookonline.com or call 1-800-WORLDBK (967-5325). For information about sales to schools and libraries, call 1-800-975-3250 (United States); 1-800-837-5365 (Canada).

2006 Revised printing

World Book, Inc.
233 N. Michigan Avenue
Chicago, IL 60601
U.S.A.

The Library of Congress has cataloged an earlier edition of this title as follows:

Iguanas and other lizards.
    p. cm. -- (World Book's animals of the world)
    Includes bibliographical references and index.
    ISBN 0-7166-1268-2
    1. Iguanas--Juvenile literature. 2. Lizards--Juvenile literature.
    I. World Book, Inc. II. Series.
    QL666 .L251369 2005
    597.95'42--dc22

                            2004015691

This edition:
Iguanas: ISBN-10: 0-7166-1299-2 ISBN-13: 978-0-7166-1299-5
Set 4: ISBN-10: 0-7166-1285-2   ISBN-13: 978-0-7166-1285-8

Printed in Malaysia
3 4 5 6 7 8 09 08 07

Picture Acknowledgments: Cover: © John Giustina, Bruce Coleman Inc.; © Joe McDonald, Animals Animals; © M.H. Sharp, Photo Researchers; © Gail Shumway, Bruce Coleman Inc.; © Norman Owen Tomalin, Bruce Coleman; Inc.

© Stephen Dalton, Photo Researchers 17; © Tim Davis, Photo Researchers 15; © E.R. Degginger, Photo Researchers 35; © Michael Fogden, Animals Animals 33; © John Giustina, Bruce Coleman Inc. 3, 61; © David Hosking, Photo Researchers 21; © Zigmund Leszczynski, Animals Animals 25, 41; © Craig K. Lorenz, Photo Researchers 55; © Joe McDonald, Animals Animals 27; © Joe McDonald, Okapia/Photo Researchers 11; © Jean-Luc Petit, Gamma Presse 5, 39; © Rod Planck, Photo Researchers 53; © James Robinson, Animals Animals 47; © Jany Sauvanet, Photo Researchers 51; © M.H. Sharp, Photo Researchers 45; © Gail Shumway, Bruce Coleman Inc. 4, 7, 31, 57; © Barbara Strnadova, Photo Researchers 49; © Dan Suzio, Photo Researchers 23; © Norman Owen Tomalin, Bruce Coleman Inc. 5, 19, 37, 43; © Dave Watts, Tom Stack & Associates 59; © Wai Ping Wu, Bruce Coleman Inc. 29.

Illustrations: WORLD BOOK illustrations by John Fleck 13, 48.

World Book's Animals of the World

Iguanas
and Other Lizards

WORLD
BOOK

a Scott Fetzer company
Chicago
www.worldbookonline.com

Contents

Who are you calling helmet-head?

Get out of the way! Let the big lizard eat!

Thinking about the dinosaur I resemble makes me laugh!

What Is a Lizard?

A lizard is a reptile. Reptiles are animals that are cold-blooded vertebrates. Cold-blooded animals do not control their own body temperature, their temperature is determined by the temperature of their surroundings. And, vertebrates are animals with a backbone.

Lizards, which are closely related to snakes, vary in size, shape, and color. Lizards' bodies are covered with scales. Each scale is a piece of thickened skin that helps protect lizards from attackers. These scales also limit the loss of heat and moisture from the lizard's body.

"Iguana" is the name given to certain types of lizard. There are about 35 different species, or kinds, of iguana. They are mainly brown, gray, or green. Some live on land, some live in trees, and some burrow in the sand. Certain iguanas, such as the marine iguana that lives in the Galapagos Islands, are very good swimmers.

6

Helmeted lizard

Where in the World Do Iguanas and Other Lizards Live?

Iguanas live in an area that stretches from southern Canada south to Argentina. A few species live on the island of Madagascar in the Indian Ocean and on the islands of Fiji and Tonga in the Pacific Ocean.

Lizards live almost everywhere except the areas near the North and South poles. They are most often found in the tropics and in warm parts of the temperate zones. These zones are the two regions of Earth between the tropics and the polar circles.

Lizards are the most common reptiles found in deserts and other dry regions. When the desert becomes too hot for comfort, lizards lie in the shade or under the sand to escape the sun's rays.

World Map

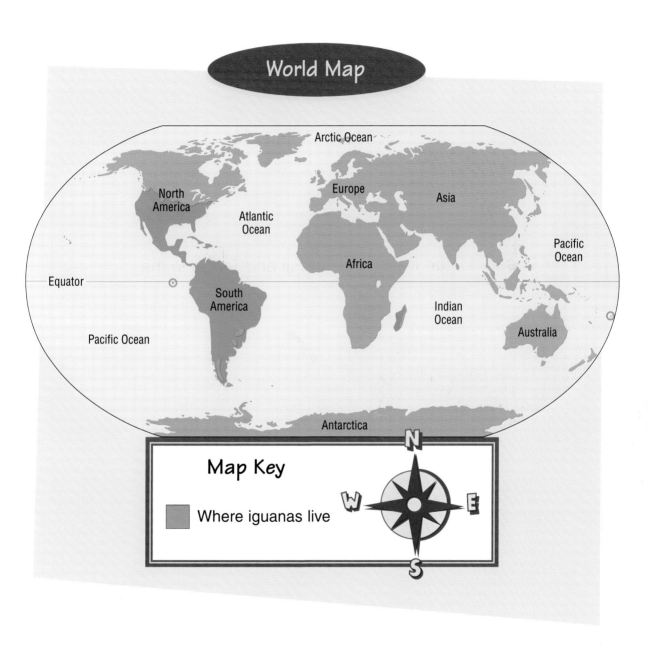

Arctic Ocean

North
America

Europe

Asia

Atlantic
Ocean

Pacific
Ocean

Africa

Equator

South
America

Indian
Ocean

Australia

Pacific Ocean

Antarctica

Map Key

Where iguanas live

N
W   E
S

9

How Do Iguanas and Other Lizards Get Around?

Most iguanas and other lizards get around by walking on their four legs. But, two types of iguana, the collared lizard of the southwestern United States and Mexico and the basilisk *(BAS uh lihsk)* of Mexico and Central America, can run using only two of their four legs. They raise the front of their body and run using their hind legs. Some basilisks can even run on water. A fringe of skin around their toes lets them skim the water's surface.

Another kind of lizard, the fringe-toed lizard, lives in the deserts of the southwestern United States and northwestern Mexico. These animals have a comblike fringe on their toes to help them run across the loose surface of the sand.

No present-day lizards can fly, but a small group called flying dragons comes close to doing that. They glide from tree to tree, as flying squirrels do. Flying dragons can spread out a fold of skin along either side of their body. They do this by moving several long ribs that support this fold of skin. This creates a "wing" that lets them sail short distances through the air.

Plumed basilisk running over water

What's Under
All Those Scales?

Under its thick skin, an iguana has many different organs, including a three-chambered heart. (The human heart has four chambers.) Some of the iguana's other organs are a well-developed pair of lungs and a pair of kidneys.

Unlike many animals, some iguanas have no urinary bladder. These iguanas turn waste liquid into a whitish substance, which passes out of the body in a solid form. This helps iguanas survive on less water.

Iguanas and other lizards have a special organ within the roof of their mouth. It is called the Jacobson's organ. This organ may help them tell whether another iguana is male or female. It also helps them test possible foods.

Iguanas also have an opening in the top of the skull covered only by skin and tissue. Beneath this opening is a structure called the "third eye." This structure seems to send signals to the brain. Scientists think the third eye may help the animal sense how long the day is and figure out how long to sunbathe.

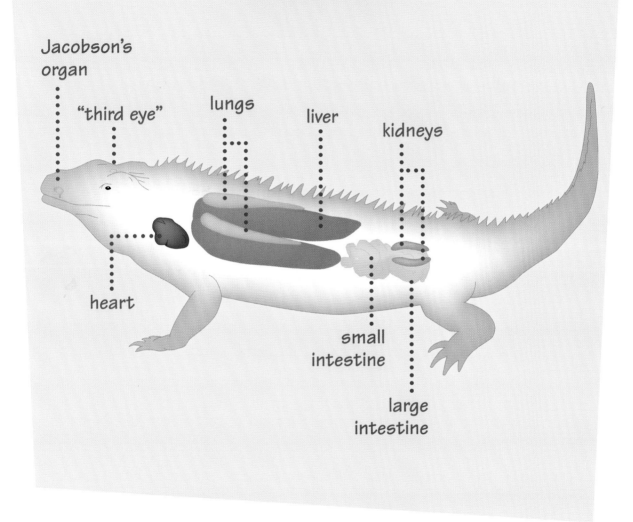

Diagram of
an Iguana

Jacobson's organ

"third eye"

lungs

liver

kidneys

heart

small intestine

large intestine

13

What's for Dinner?

Iguanas eat insects, fruit, flowers, and leaves. Some iguanas will even eat cactus plants.

Most lizards have trouble digesting plants—that is, breaking the plants down into nutrients that their bodies can use. Bacteria, tiny single-celled organisms, in the iguana's digestive system help it to digest plants. Iguanas do not have these bacteria when they hatch. Scientists think iguanas may get these bacteria by eating the feces (*FEE seez*, meaning digestive wastes) of adult iguanas.

Iguanas are plant-eaters, but many lizards, such as the Komodo dragon, are meat-eaters. The Komodo dragon even eats animals as large as deer and water buffaloes.

Galapagos land iguana eating a cactus

Why Might Common Iguanas Become "Uncommon"?

Green iguanas, also known as common iguanas, are found in a range from Mexico to southern Brazil and Paraguay. They may grow up to 6 feet (1.8 meters) long.

Green iguanas live in trees, especially near water. To avoid being seen, they stay very still in tree branches. Their coloring blends in with the branches. If an enemy does attack, these lizards leap out of the trees and hide underwater.

People often eat these iguanas and their eggs. In fact, the green iguana's Spanish name, *gallina de palo*, means "chicken of the tree"—a name given to them because they are so tasty.

Also, people often capture these lizards to sell as pets. As a result, common iguanas are in danger of becoming uncommon in some of their wild habitats.

Green, or common, iguanas

What Type of Iguana Lives in the Sea?

The Galapagos marine iguana lives in the sea. It is the only lizard that does so. This iguana lives on the Galapagos Islands, located off the coast of Ecuador.

Marine iguanas are found along coastal rocks, where they dive underwater to search for algae *(AL jee)* to eat. Algae are plantlike organisms that do not have stems, roots, or leaves. Another name for algae that grow in the ocean is seaweed.

Marine iguanas end up taking in a lot of salt because the algae they eat grow in salt water. To clear the salt out of their noses, marine iguanas sneeze and snort often. The salt they sneeze out lands atop their heads. This can make them look like they are wearing old-fashioned powdered wigs!

Marine iguanas, which are expert swimmers, must go into the sea for long periods to get enough food. They use their flattened tails to help them swim.

A marine iguana sports a white salt "wig"

Can Marine Iguanas "Shrink"?

Galapagos marine iguanas can shrink in size by as much as one-fifth when food is scarce. If a change in climate reduces the supply of the lizards' favorite foods, the lizards may respond by becoming smaller. That way, they do not need as much food. These iguanas can become as much as 2 ¾ inches (7 centimeters) shorter "from snout to vent" (a way that scientists usually measure them) when necessary. The animals' bones actually become smaller during these periods. Marine iguanas can grow back to their larger size again when there is plenty of food.

The marine iguana is the first vertebrate species known to reduce the size of its bones to adapt to changing conditions. Scientists are interested in studying this process because they hope it will help them solve such human health problems as osteoporosis *(os tee oh puh ROH sis)*, a condition in which bones become very fragile.

Galapagos marine
iguanas

Why Do Iguanas Sunbathe?

Iguanas and other lizards are cold-blooded, which means they do not produce their own body heat. They need outside sources of heat to keep warm. The most important of these sources is the sun. So, iguanas spend much of their time bathing in the sunlight.

If it is a cold time of year and their temperature falls too low, the lizards become sluggish. Their body systems begin to slow down, and they must find shelter and hibernate.

On the other hand, if a lizard becomes too hot, it cannot function properly either. It may even die from being overheated. During extremely hot periods, iguanas will seek cooler, shaded places.

Desert iguana
sunbathing

When Does an Iguana Get New Skin?

Iguanas and other lizards shed their skin as they grow. The outer layer of skin is not expandable, so it cannot grow with the animal.

Many reptiles, including snakes, shed their skin. Most snakes shed their skin in one long piece. But lizards shed their skin in patches and pieces. Some lizards speed the shedding process by pulling on the loose outer skin with their mouth or their claws.

Young iguanas shed their skin more often than older iguanas. The young first shed soon after hatching. They shed again at other times depending on their growth rate, what they eat, the temperature of the air, the amount of moisture in the air, and their health.

When an iguana sheds, it does not lose all of its skin. Like other vertebrates, iguanas actually have layered skin. As the iguana's outer layer of skin is shed, there is a new layer beneath that is ready to become the outer layer.

Jamaican giant anole
lizard shedding its skin

Why Does an Iguana Stick Out Its Tongue?

When an iguana sticks out its tongue, it is learning about its environment. Taste buds on the iguana's tongue and in its mouth give the animal clues about its surroundings.

An iguana also learns about its environment by using two tiny cavities (holes) that are located in the roof of its mouth. Together, these cavities are called Jacobson's organ. The iguana picks up particles from the air and the ground with its tongue and puts them into this organ. The cavities are lined with sensitive cells that aid the sense of smell. Nerves in the cavities send information about the particles directly to the iguana's brain.

Other lizards and snakes also have the Jacobson's organ. All these animals use this organ and their tongue to track prey, test food, and identify if another animal is male or female.

Green iguana

Why Do Some Iguanas Puff Up Like Balloons?

Chuckwallas *(CHUHK wol uhs)* are members of the iguana family. These large lizards are found in rocky deserts in the southwestern United States and in Mexico. Chuckwallas get their name from the word *chacahuala*, the Spanish name for this lizard.

When chased by a predator, a chuckwalla will run to a crack in a rock or some other narrow opening and wedge itself in tightly by filling its lungs with air. This makes it almost impossible for the predator to pry it loose!

Unlike most lizards, but like other iguanas, chuckwallas are plant-eaters. The chuckwalla's favorite foods are leaves and flowers.

Chuckwallas are the second-largest lizard in North America. Only the Gila monster is larger. The largest type of chuckwalla can grow to about 24 inches (61 centimeters) long and weigh about 2 pounds (0.9 kilograms).

Chuckwalla

Which Are the Smallest Members of the Iguana Family?

Anoles *(uh NOH leez)* are the smallest members of the iguana family. Most grow to about 8 inches (20 centimeters) long. Because of their size and many other differences, many scientists classify anoles into their own separate family.

Most anoles are green or brown and may have brightly colored patterns on their skin. Some can change their color quickly, as a chameleon can.

Like some other lizards, such as green iguanas, male anoles have a large, colorful throat flap called a dewlap. They fan their dewlap when they want to attract females or scare off rival males. Each species of anole fans its flap in a particular pattern.

The smallest lizard species is the dwarf gecko. This tiny lizard was discovered in 2001 on Isla Beata, off the coast of the Dominican Republic. The dwarf gecko is around ½ inch (some 1.25 centimeters) long.

An anole lizard
with a ladybug

What's All That Head-bobbing About?

Head-bobbing is a way that lizards communicate. Male anoles nod their heads up and down to signal to other anoles that they are males and to chase off other males at mating time.

Bobbing sometimes means a male is ready to fight another animal. It also can mean that the animal is defending its territory.

Some lizards do "push-ups" for the same reason. They push up with their front legs, which may make them look larger to an opponent.

Each species of lizard has its own pattern of head-bobbing and push-ups. This is one way in which lizards can tell which individuals belong to their own species.

Other ways in which lizards communicate include waving their tails, opening their jaws wide, changing their colors, sticking out their dewlaps, or showing off their brightly colored undersides.

Blue-eyed anole
displaying its dewlap

What Are the Dangers for Lizards' Eggs in a Nest?

Most lizard eggs are not waterproof. The shells have to be able to let moisture in so that the growing lizards can get the moisture they need to develop and hatch properly. The female lizards often lay their eggs in damp soil, fallen leaves, and rotting wood, all of which have the necessary moisture. Even sand can be a safe place for a nest, if the lizard digs down far enough to reach some water.

After laying their eggs, most females leave them alone to develop and hatch. The eggs are easy targets for other animals—they make the perfect snack! In most species of lizard, the eggs are white and are easy for animals to spot in a nest that is not well hidden. In some Central and South American countries, people eat lizard eggs.

Most female lizards lay eggs. But the females of some species give birth to live young. Among lizards that do lay eggs, most eggs require several weeks or even a few months to hatch. The eggs of a panther chameleon may need 240 or more days to develop before hatching.

34

Green iguana
with a nest of eggs

35

Which Is the Largest Living Lizard?

The Komodo dragon is the largest living lizard in the world. It grows to more than 10 feet (3 meters) long. A Komodo dragon can weigh as much as 365 pounds (166 kilograms)—much more than an average adult human!

Scientists think that the Komodo dragons' environment may be one reason the animals have become so large. Komodo dragons live on only a few Indonesian islands, where the Komodos are the largest meat-eating animals. So, a living Komodo dragon seldom becomes supper for another animal. And it does not have to compete very much for its own supper.

The Komodo dragon mainly eats dead animals, but it also hunts, kills, and eats large prey. It has been known to eat deer, wild pigs, goats, and water buffaloes. Adults will sometimes eat young Komodo dragons, too. Komodo dragons have even killed a small number of people!

Komodo dragons

Which Lizard Has Its Own National Park?

The Komodo dragon has its own national park. Komodo National Park is located on the islands of Komodo, Rinca, and Padar and many other smaller islands. These islands are part of the country of Indonesia in Southeast Asia. When the park was created in 1980, it was meant to protect just the Komodo dragon. But now the park protects all the plant and animal life in the region, both on land and in water.

The Komodo dragon is a rare species. It could become extinct if not protected. There are 5,000 to 6,000 of these lizards left in the wild. They can be exported to other countries only with the permission of Indonesia's president, and then only as a gift to another nation.

Komodo dragon in
Komodo National Park

39

What Color Is a Chameleon?

A chameleon is able to change its skin color quickly. This lizard may be green, yellow, or white one minute, and brown or black the next. Chameleons also may become spotted. The chameleon's color is controlled by body chemicals called hormones *(HAWR mohnz)*.

Many people believe chameleons change color to blend with their surroundings in order to hide from predators. This, however, is not true. Chameleons actually change their color depending on the air temperature or the amount of light, though most often the animal changes color because of its mood.

The skin of a chameleon is see-through, or transparent. The chameleon has cells underneath this skin that contain pigment (a natural substance that controls the color of tissues in animals). By increasing the size of certain pigment cells and decreasing the size of other pigment cells, the chameleon changes color. For instance, if a chameleon decreases the size of its black-pigment cells and increases the size of its yellow, its skin changes from black to yellow.

Chameleons displaying
fighting colors

Which Chameleon Looks Like a *Triceratops?*

A male Jackson's chameleon has three ridged horns on its head. One horn is on the lizard's snout and the other two are above its eyes. The horns make this lizard look something like the dinosaur *Triceratops (try SEHR uh tops)*, whose name means three-horned face.

Male Jackson's chameleons use their horns when they fight other males over territory or possible mates. When they fight, the males use their horns the way a medieval knight used a lance while jousting. These chameleons may also use their horns to help attract mates. And scientists think the horns help Jackson's chameleons recognize others of their own species.

Female Jackson's chameleons do not have fully developed horns. They have only three small lumps or a single spike on their head.

Male Jackson's chameleon

Which Lizard Is Often Mistaken for a Snake?

Glass lizards are often mistaken for snakes. These lizards have no legs, and they are long and slender in shape. They are called glass lizards because their tails are very brittle and can easily snap off.

Many people call these lizards glass snakes. But, if you look closely, you'll see that glass lizards have ear openings and movable eyelids. Snakes do not.

Glass lizards live in the southeastern and central parts of the United States and in Mexico, Europe, Asia, and Africa. Some of these lizards grow to be about 2 feet (0.6 meter) long, with tails that are twice as long as their bodies. There are 14 species, or types, of glass lizard.

Some other species of lizard, including several species of skink, have no legs or very weak, small legs. These lizards usually live in the sand or on the ground, where they do not need legs to climb and cling to tree branches.

Glass lizard

45

What Trick Can Glass Lizards Do With Their Tail?

A glass lizard's tail is very fragile, or easily broken. A predator can snap off the glass lizard's tail during an attack. But this can actually be a good thing. The tail can wriggle for a short time after breaking off. This may distract the attacker and allow the glass lizard to escape. The lizard does not seem to miss its tail. In time it grows a new, shorter tail.

Several other kinds of lizard, including geckos and skinks, can break off their tail and grow a new one. The same lizard can lose its tail many times and grow a new one after each loss! The new tail may be shorter and fatter, and may have different markings. It begins to grow right after the old tail is snapped off.

Lizards' tails are used for many other things in addition to defense. They help the lizards balance while walking or running. They store fat, which can be used when food is scarce. And, some lizards also use their tails as an "extra leg" to grasp branches while they climb.

46

Glass lizards (top tail shows regeneration)

47

How Do Geckos Walk on the Ceiling?

Scientists used to think that geckos had disks on their toes that worked like suction cups. But now we know that it is the hairs on the underside of these lizards' toes that help the animals climb and cling.

The toes of most geckos end with pads that have thousands of tiny, stiff hairs. These hairs stick to most surfaces, making the animals good climbers. Some geckos can walk upside down on the underside of a branch, ceiling, or other flat surface.

Since geckos' feet stick to whatever surface they are on, why don't these hairs prevent the lizards from walking and jumping? Because, luckily, geckos have a way to keep from getting stuck in place. Each of a gecko's toes can be curled away from the surface it is on. This loosens the clinging hairs and allows the animal to move.

underside of
gecko's foot
and toes

Tokay gecko walking
on the ceiling

Which Species of Lizard Have Only Female Offspring?

Most animals, including lizards, need both a female and a male to mate in order to reproduce, or have offspring. But the females of about 30 species of lizard can reproduce when a male is not present. The offspring of these lizards are all female. A single female lizard is able to lay eggs or give birth to young lizards that are clones of (genetically identical to) their mother. The females of 10 species of whiptail lizard from the southwestern United States and Mexico are among those who reproduce without males.

There are pluses and minuses to being able to reproduce without a male. One good thing is that the lizards do not need to spend time finding or fighting over mates. Because of this, a group can increase in size quickly. But one bad thing is that the offspring are genetically identical to their mother (and to each other). Genetic diversity is good for a species. It gives a species a better chance of adapting to different or changing environments.

Spotted whiptail lizard

Why Are Some Lizards Mistaken for Toads?

Horned lizards are often mistaken for toads because their bodies have a flattened, toadlike shape. In fact, many people call them horned toads or horny toads. But they are reptiles, not amphibians as toads are.

Horned lizards grow from 2 ½ to 6 ½ inches (6.4 to 16.5 centimeters) long. Their bodies are covered with sharp spines. Large spines stick out from the backs of their head. Their spiny armor protects them from animals that attack them.

Some horned lizards have an unusual way of defending themselves. They can squirt blood from their eyes to ward off an attacker! The blood can travel as far as 4 feet (1.2 meters). Not surprisingly, if an attacker is hit in the face with this blood, it often becomes frightened and runs away.

Short-horned lizard

Are Lizards Poisonous?

Only two species of lizards are known to be poisonous. They are the Gila *(HEE luh)* monster and the Mexican beaded lizard. Their bites are painful, but rarely deadly, to healthy humans.

Gila monsters and Mexican beaded lizards use their poisonous bite mostly to defend themselves against other creatures. These lizards are immune to their own poison, which is called venom. This means that their bites do not kill others of their own species.

The Gila monster was probably named for the Gila River in Arizona. These lizards are found from the southwestern United States to northwestern Mexico. Mexican beaded lizards live along the Pacific coast of Mexico and Guatemala. Both kinds of lizards spend most of their time underground. In fact, scientists think Gila monsters may spend 98 percent of their time (that is about as much as 23 ½ hours a day) in their underground burrows. They leave their burrows mainly in the evening, when the desert air is cooler.

Gila monster

Do Lizards Have Many Ways to Defend Themselves?

Yes, lizards defend themselves in many ways.

The most common self-defense for a lizard is running away. But some lizards do the opposite: they freeze when they see an enemy, counting on their camouflage colors or bright patterns to help hide them. A few species of lizards even "play dead." These lizards hope they will not be interesting to a predator if that predator thinks they are already dead.

Just as the glass lizard uses its tail to distract an attacker, other lizards also bluff, or play tricks. Some try to look more fierce than they are by lashing their tails, hissing, or puffing out their bodies to look larger.

Some lizards, including monitors, use their jaws for biting. They clamp their jaws and sink their teeth into an attacker's body and then hang on. Even a lizard that is not poisonous can do a lot of damage by biting its enemy.

Camouflaged gecko

Which Lizard Looks Like It Wears a Ruffled Collar?

The frilled lizard has a flap of loose skin around its neck. When the lizard is calm, it keeps the flap of skin folded close to its body. But when the lizard is alarmed by another animal, it hisses loudly, rears up on its back legs, shows the bright yellow lining of its mouth, and expands this colorful frill, or flap, of skin.

To humans, this makes the lizard look like it is wearing a fancy ruffled collar. But to other animals, it is supposed to make the lizard look much bigger and more fierce than it is. If this does not discourage a predator, the lizard then runs off quickly on its hind legs, with its forelegs and tail raised.

The frilled lizard lives in tropical northern Australia. It grows to about 3 feet (1 meter) long. Its extended collar may measure 9 inches (23 centimeters) around.

Bearded lizards have many long, pointed scales covering their throats. When they are threatened, these lizards open their mouths wide and inflate their throats. This makes their scales stick up, which scares away their enemies.

58

Frilled lizard

Are Lizards in Danger?

Some species of lizard are endangered, and others are threatened. In many areas, the lizards' habitats have been destroyed. Forests have been cut down, roads have been built, and wetlands have been drained or dammed.

In the past, some lizards were killed for their skins. These skins were used to make wallets, handbags, and other products. But many countries now forbid killing lizards for this purpose. In some countries, people still kill lizards to eat, or eat the lizards' eggs.

Marine iguanas are threatened by oil spills near their home in the Galapagos Islands. There was a bad oil spill near the Galapagos Islands in 2001. The next year, scientists said that about 15,000 marine iguanas had died on a nearby island.

More than two dozen species of lizards are officially called endangered, and many more are considered vulnerable. Among the endangered species are the Fiji crested iguana, the Coachella Valley fringe-toed lizard, and a legless species of skink.

Fiji crested iguana

→ Some geckos have claws that they can draw in as a cat does.

→ Several types of geckos can shed their entire skin at once when handled or grabbed. This lets them slip away from whatever is trying to catch them.

→ The tongue of a chameleon may be as long as the animal's entire body. The tongue shoots out of the chameleon's mouth so rapidly that the human eye can hardly see it.

→ Armadillo lizards and sungazers defend themselves by grasping their tails in their jaws. Their tails are covered with sharp spines, and the lizards use them to protect their bellies, which otherwise could be easily attacked.

→ The ancient Egyptians made mummies of desert lizards.

→ The six-lined racerunner can run for short distances at 18 miles (29 kilometers) per hour.

Glossary

algae Simple, plantlike organisms that usually live in water.

camouflage Features of an animal, such as skin coloring, that help it blend into its surroundings.

clone An organism that is genetically identical to another organism.

cold-blooded Having a body temperature that stays the same as the air temperature.

dewlap The flap of skin around the neck of some lizards.

digestion The breaking down of food into smaller bits that the body can use for energy.

fertility The ability to reproduce, or have offspring.

genes Tiny structures inside cells that determine which traits an individual gets from its parents.

head-bobbing A form of communication between lizards in which their heads move up and down.

hibernate When an animal spends a period or a season in a state of deep sleep; often, the animal's metabolism and body temperature are lowered when hibernating.

hormone A body chemical that influences various functions inside the body.

immune To be protected from a disease or poison.

Jacobson's organ A pair of tiny structures in the roof of the mouth of some reptiles that helps them smell and taste.

reptiles A group of cold-blooded animals that have scaly skin and usually reproduce by laying eggs.

temperate zone Region of Earth between the hot, tropical regions and the cold, polar regions.

vertebrate An animal with a backbone.

Index

(**Boldface** indicates a photo, map, or illustration.)

For more information about Iguanas and Other Lizards, try these resources:

Desert Iguanas, by Judith Jango-Cohen, Lerner Publications, 2001.

Iguanas, by Sandra Donovan, Raintree, 2002.

Lizards: A Natural History of Some Uncommon Creatures, by David Badger, Voyageur Press, 2003.

http://animaldiversity.ummz.umich.edu/site/accounts/information/Iguanidae.html

http://www.darwinfoundation.org/terrest/iguana2.html

http://www.greenigsociety.org/inthewild.htm

http://www.sandiegozoo.org/animalbytes/t-iguana.html

Iguana Classification

Scientists classify animals by placing them into groups. The animal kingdom is a group that contains all the world's animals. Phylum, class, order, and family are smaller groups. Each phylum contains many classes. A class contains orders, an order contains families, and a family contains individual species. Each species also has its own scientific name. (The abbreviation "spp." after a genus name indicates that a group of species from a genus is being discussed.) Here is how the animals in this book fit into this system.

Animals with backbones and their relatives (Phylum Chordata)

Reptiles (Class Reptilia)

Lizards and snakes (Order Squamata)

Beaded lizards (Family Helodermatidae)
Mexican beaded lizard . . . .*Heloderma horridum*
Gila monster . . . .*Heloderma suspectum*

Casque-headed lizards (Family Corytophanidae)
Helmeted lizards . . . .*Corytophanes* spp.

Chameleons (Family Chamaeleonidae)
Jackson's chameleon . . . .*Chamaeleo jacksonii*
Panther chameleon . . . .*Chamaeleo (furcifer) pardalis*

Geckoes (Family Gekkonidae)
Dwarf gecko . . . .*Sphaerodactylus ariasae*
Tokay gecko . . . .*Gekko gecko*

Glass lizards and their relatives (Family Anguidae)
Glass lizards . . . .*Ophisaurus* spp.

Girdle-tailed lizards (Family Cordylidae)
Armadillo lizard . . . .*Cordylus cataphractus*
Sungazer . . . .*Cordylus giganteus*

Iguanas and their relatives (Family Iguanidae)
Anoles . . . .*Anolis* spp. *
Basilisks . . . .*Basiliscus* spp. **
Chuckwallas . . . .*Sauromalus* spp.
Coachella Valley fringe-toed lizard . . . .*Uma inornata* ***
Collared lizards . . . .*Crotaphytus* spp.****
Desert iguana . . . .*Dipsosaurus dorsalis*
Fiji crested iguana . . . .*Brachylophus vitiensis*
Galapagos land iguana . . . .*Conolophus subcristatus*
Galapagos marine iguana . . . .*Amblyrhynchus cristatus*
Green, or common, iguana . . . .*Iguana iguana*
Horned lizards . . . .*Phrynosoma* spp.***

Monitor lizards (Family Varanidae)
Komodo dragon . . . .*Varanus komodoensis*

Old World lizards (Family Agamidae)
Bearded lizard . . . .*Pogona vitticeps*
Flying dragons . . . .*Draco* spp.
Frilled lizard . . . .*Chlamydosaurus kingii*

Skinks (Family Scincidae)

Whiptails (Family Teiidae)
Six-lined racerunner . . . .*Cnemidophorus sexlineatus*
Spotted whiptail . . . .*Cnemidophorus exsanguis*

* Some scientists classify certain of these lizards under the genus *Norops*. May also be grouped in the family Polychrotidae.
** May be grouped into the family Corytophanidae.
*** May be grouped into the family Phrynosomatidae.
**** May be grouped into the family Crotaphytidae.